Simple

Healthy
Eating

p

This ia a Parragon book

This edition published in 2005

Parragon
Queen Street House
4 Queen Street
Bath BA1 1HE
United Kingdom

ISBN: 1-40546-213-2

Printed in Indonesia

This edition designed by Shelley Doyle

Photography and text by The Bridgewater Book Company Ltd

Cover Photography by Mark Wood

Cover Home Economist Pamela Gwyther

NOTES FOR THE READER

This book uses both metric and imperial measurements. Follow the same units of measurement throughout; do not mix metric and imperial.

All spoon measurements are level: teaspoons are assumed to be 5 ml, and tablespoons are assumed to be 15 ml.

Unless otherwise stated, milk is assumed to be full fat and eggs are medium.

Recipes using raw or very lightly cooked eggs should be avoided by infants, the elderly, pregnant women, convalescents and anyone suffering from an illness.

Optional ingredients, variations or serving suggestions have not been included in the calculations. The times given are an approximate guide only. Preparation times differ according to the techniques used by different people and the cooking times may also vary from those given.

contents

introduction

Low-fat good, high-fat bad – but what exactly this means and how you can translate this message into appetizing, easy-to-cook, healthy meals is not so straightforward. The good news is that it is possible to cook delicious dishes that all the family will enjoy without spending huge amounts of time shopping, cooking and, most off-putting of all, checking endless labels and nutritional charts.

The key to a nutritious diet and to healthy eating in general is to use carefully selected, fresh ingredients. While low-fat ready-meals can help, they tend to be more expensive than cooking for yourself and may contain a high proportion of other unwanted ingredients, such as salt and sugar. By cooking 'from scratch', you know exactly what and how much of anything has gone into a dish. As an added bonus, really fresh ingredients are packed with essential vitamins and minerals, as well as cancer-busting antioxidants and other health-enhancing substances. What's more, fresh food tastes great.

The majority of the recipes in this book contain no more than 7 grams of fat per serving and many have even less. It features interesting, tasty and satisfying dishes from around the world, suitable for all courses, seasons and occasions. They use everyday ingredients that won't break the housekeeping budget and – best news of all for the family cook – the techniques that work best for healthy cooking are the easiest and often the quickest.

Low-fat food has an undeserved reputation for being tasteless. If this still needs disproving, the following recipes will do away with this myth once and for all. Soups, stir-fries, pizza, curries, kebabs and desserts offer a wealth of choice, so there is sure to be something to suit everyone. Subtle use of spices and herbs, clever combinations of complementary ingredients and using foods that are naturally low in fat, especially the very unhealthy saturated fats, will set the taste buds tingling.

starters
and
light bites

This chapter offers you delicious starters, snacks, and even light lunches. Low-fat food doesn't need to be low on inspiration. Dishes like Parma Ham with Figs, or Prawn and Mango Salad, could form an exotic and tasty weekday lunch or, equally, a stunning starter to a dinner party.

tuna and fresh vegetable salad

extremely easy

prep 10 mins + 1 hr to marinate

cooking 0 mins

NUTRITIONAL INFORMATION	
calories	187
fat	6g
saturates	0.5g

DRESSING

4 tbsp reduced-calorie mayonnaise

4 tbsp low-fat natural yogurt

2 tbsp white wine vinegar

salt and pepper

12 cherry tomatoes, halved

225 g/8 oz whole green beans, cut into 2.5 cm/ 1 inch pieces

225 g/8 oz courgettes, sliced thinly

225 g/8 oz button mushrooms, sliced thinly

350 g/12 oz canned tuna in brine, drained and flaked

chopped fresh parsley, to garnish

salad leaves, to serve

SERVES 4

To make the dressing, put the mayonnaise, yogurt, vinegar, salt and pepper in a screw-topped jar and shake together until the ingredients are well blended.

Put the tomatoes, beans, courgettes and mushrooms in a bowl. Pour over the dressing and leave to marinate for about 1 hour.

To serve, arrange the salad leaves on a serving dish. Add the vegetables and then the tuna and garnish with chopped parsley.

extremely easy

prep 10 mins

cooking 0 mins

prawn and mango salad

2 mangoes

225 g/8 oz peeled, cooked
  prawns

DRESSING

juice from the mangoes

6 tbsp low-fat natural yogurt

2 tbsp reduced-calorie
  mayonnaise

1 tbsp lemon juice

salt and pepper

salad leaves, to serve

4 whole cooked prawns,
  to garnish

NUTRITIONAL INFORMATION	
calories	146
fat	3g
saturates	0.5g

SERVES 4

Cutting close to the stone, cut a large slice from one side of
each mango, then cut another slice from the opposite side.
Without breaking the skin, cut the flesh in the segments into
squares, then push the skin inside out to expose the cubes
and cut away from the skin. Use a sharp knife to peel the
remaining centre section and cut the flesh away from the
stone into cubes. Reserve any juice in a bowl and put the
mango flesh in a separate bowl.

Add the prawns to the mango flesh. To the juice, add the
yogurt, mayonnaise, lemon juice, salt and pepper and
blend together.

Arrange the salad leaves on a serving dish and add the
mango flesh and prawns. Pour over the dressing and serve
garnished with the whole prawns.

parma ham with figs

extremely easy

**prep 10 mins +
20 mins to chill**

cooking 0 mins

*175 g/6 oz Parma ham,
     thinly sliced*

pepper

4 fresh figs

1 lime

2 fresh basil sprigs

NUTRITIONAL INFORMATION	
calories	124
fat	6g
saturates	2g

SERVES 4

Using a sharp knife, trim the visible fat from the slices of ham and discard. Arrange the ham on 4 large serving plates, loosely folding it so that it falls into decorative shapes. Season to taste with pepper.

Using a sharp knife, cut each fig lengthways into 4 wedges. Arrange a fig on each serving plate. Cut the lime into 6 wedges, place a wedge on each plate and reserve the others. Remove the leaves from the basil sprigs and divide between the plates. Cover with clingfilm and leave in the refrigerator to chill until ready to serve.

Just before serving, remove the plates from the refrigerator and squeeze the juice from the remaining lime wedges over the ham.

very easy

prep 10 mins

cooking 20 mins

speedy broccoli soup

350 g/12 oz broccoli

1 leek, sliced

1 celery stick, sliced

1 garlic clove, crushed

350 g/12 oz potato, diced

1 litre/1³/₄ pints vegetable
  stock

1 bay leaf

freshly ground black pepper

crusty bread or toasted
  croûtons, to serve

SERVES 6

Cut the broccoli into florets and set aside. Cut the thicker
broccoli stalks into 1-cm/¹/₂-inch dice and put into a large
saucepan with the leek, celery, garlic, potato, stock and bay
leaf. Bring to the boil, then reduce the heat, cover and simmer
for 15 minutes

Add the broccoli florets to the soup and return to the boil.
Reduce the heat, cover and simmer for a further 3–5 minutes,
or until the potato and broccoli stalks are tender.

Remove from the heat and leave the soup to cool slightly.
Remove and discard the bay leaf. Purée the soup, in small
batches, in a food processor or blender until smooth.

Return the soup to the saucepan and heat through thoroughly.
Season to taste with pepper. Ladle the soup into warmed
bowls and serve immediately with crusty bread or toasted
croûtons.

NUTRITIONAL INFORMATION	
calories	140
fat	1.3g
saturates	0.27g

chicken wraps

very easy

prep 10 mins

cooking 0 mins

150 g/5¹/₂ oz low-fat natural yogurt

1 tbsp wholegrain mustard

freshly ground black pepper

280 g/10 oz cooked skinless, boneless chicken breast, diced

140 g/5 oz iceberg lettuce, finely shredded

85 g/3 oz cucumber, thinly sliced

2 celery sticks, sliced

85 g/3 oz black seedless grapes, halved

8 x 20-cm/8-inch soft flour tortillas or 4 x 25-cm/ 10-inch soft flour tortillas

NUTRITIONAL INFORMATION

calories	269
fat	2.6g
saturates	0.7g

SERVES 4

Combine the yogurt and mustard in a bowl and season to taste with pepper. Stir in the chicken and toss until thoroughly coated.

Put the lettuce, cucumber, celery and grapes into a separate bowl and mix well.

Fold a tortilla in half and in half again to make a cone that is easy to hold. Half-fill the tortilla pocket with the salad mixture and top with some of the chicken mixture. Repeat with the remaining tortillas, salad and chicken. Serve immediately.

meat
and
poultry

Despite much bad press meat provides essential energy and nutrients and is delicious when good quality, fresh, lean meat is used. Poultry is a fantastic low-fat food, versatile and tasty too. Get great satisfaction from Sausage and Lentil Stew or superb Moroccan-Style Turkey with Apricots.

mexican chicken burritos

very easy

prep 10 mins

cooking 30 mins

8 wheat flour tortillas

vegetable oil spray

1 onion, chopped finely

4 boneless chicken breasts,
  skinned and sliced thinly

1 packet taco seasoning

4 tomatoes, chopped roughly

4 spring onions, sliced finely

1 tub tomato salsa, to serve

SERVES 4

Preheat the oven to 150°C/300°F/Gas Mark 2.

Wrap the tortillas in aluminium foil and cook in the oven for 10 minutes, or until soft.

Meanwhile, spray a large non-stick frying pan with oil. Add the onion and cook for 5 minutes, or until softened. Add the chicken. Stirring occasionally, cook for 5 minutes, or until tender. Stir in the taco seasoning.

Preheat the oven to 180°C/350°F/Gas Mark 4. Put the chicken mixture in the centre of each tortilla and add the tomatoes and spring onions. Fold the tortillas into a parcel and put in an ovenproof dish.

Cover the dish and cook in the preheated oven for 20 minutes. Spoon the tomato salsa over the hot tortillas before serving.

NUTRITIONAL INFORMATION	
calories	473
fat	4g
saturates	1g

easy

prep 5 mins

cooking 1 hr

sausage and lentil stew

55 g/2 oz chorizo sausage,
  very thinly sliced

1 onion, finely chopped

225 g/8 oz Puy lentils

600 ml/1 pint chicken stock

400 ml/14 fl oz water

1 carrot, thinly sliced

1 celery stick, thinly sliced

2 tsp chopped fresh parsley

salt and pepper

SERVES 4

Reserve a few slices of chorizo for the garnish and cut the remaining slices into thin strips. Dry-fry the slices and strips in a frying pan over a low heat, stirring frequently, for 2–3 minutes. Remove the chorizo slices and reserve. Add the onion to the frying pan and cook, stirring occasionally, for a further 5 minutes, or until softened.

Transfer the onion to a large, heavy-based saucepan. Add the lentils, chicken stock and water and bring to the boil over a medium heat. Cover and simmer for 30–40 minutes, or until the lentils are tender.

Add the carrot, celery and parsley and season to taste with salt and pepper. Cover and simmer for a further 8–10 minutes, or until the carrot is tender. Serve immediately, garnished with the reserved chorizo slices.

NUTRITIONAL INFORMATION	
calories	217
fat	4g
saturates	1g

stir-fried beef and mangetouts

*450 g/1 lb rump or sirloin
    steak, sliced thinly*

2 tbsp soy sauce

5 tbsp hoisin sauce

2 tbsp dry sherry

vegetable oil spray

1 onion, sliced thinly

1 tsp chopped fresh garlic

1 tsp chopped fresh ginger

1 carrot, sliced thinly

450 g/1 lb mangetouts

*225 g/8 oz canned sliced
    bamboo shoots, drained*

*fresh sprigs of coriander,
    to garnish*

*cooked rice or noodles,
    to serve*

NUTRITIONAL INFORMATION	
calories	249
fat	6g
saturates	2g

SERVES 4

Put the strips of beef in a bowl, add the soy sauce, hoisin sauce and sherry and stir together. Leave to marinate whilst cooking the vegetables.

Spray a large non-stick wok with oil. Add the onion, garlic, ginger, carrot and mangetouts and stir-fry for 5 minutes, or until softened.

Add the beef and marinade to the wok and stir-fry for 2–3 minutes, or until tender. Add the bamboo shoots and stir-fry for a further minute, until hot.

Transfer to a warm serving dish, garnish with coriander and serve with cooked rice or noodles, if desired.

easy

prep 10 mins

cooking 35 mins

moroccan-style turkey with apricots

400 g/14 oz skinless, boneless turkey breast, diced

1 onion, sliced

1 tsp ground cumin

$^1/_2$ tsp ground cinnamon

1 tsp hot chilli pepper sauce

240 g/8$^1/_2$ oz canned chickpeas, drained

600 ml/1 pint chicken stock

12 dried apricots

40 g/1$^1/_2$ oz cornflour

75 ml/2$^1/_2$ fl oz cold water

2 tbsp chopped fresh coriander

cooked couscous, rice or jacket sweet potatoes, to serve

SERVES 4

Put the turkey, onion, cumin, cinnamon, chilli pepper sauce, chickpeas and stock into a large saucepan and bring to the boil, then reduce the heat, cover and simmer for 15 minutes.

Stir in the apricots and return to the boil. Reduce the heat, cover and simmer for a further 15 minutes, or until the turkey is thoroughly cooked and tender.

Blend the cornflour with the water in a small bowl and stir into the casserole. Return to the boil, stirring constantly, and cook until the casserole thickens. Reduce the heat, cover and simmer for a further 5 minutes.

Stir half the coriander into the casserole. Transfer to a warmed serving dish and sprinkle over the remaining coriander. Serve immediately with cooked couscous, rice or jacket sweet potatoes.

NUTRITIONAL INFORMATION	
calories	387
fat	4.7g
saturates	1.3g

sticky lime chicken

very easy

prep 5 mins

cooking 40 mins

4 part-boned, skinless chicken breasts, about 140 g/5 oz each

grated rind and juice of 1 lime

1 tbsp clear honey

1 tbsp olive oil

1 garlic clove, chopped (optional)

1 tbsp chopped fresh thyme

freshly ground black pepper

boiled new potatoes and lightly cooked vegetables, to serve

NUTRITIONAL INFORMATION	
calories	203
fat	5.3g
saturates	1g

SERVES 4

Preheat the oven to 190°C/375°F/Gas Mark 5. Arrange the chicken breasts in a shallow roasting tin.

Put the lime rind and juice, honey, oil, garlic, if using, and thyme in a small bowl and combine thoroughly. Spoon the mixture evenly over the chicken breasts and season with pepper.

Roast the chicken in the preheated oven, basting every 10 minutes, for 35–40 minutes, or until the chicken is tender and the juices run clear when a skewer is inserted into the thickest part of the meat. If the juices still run pink, return the chicken to the oven and cook for a further 5 minutes, then re-test. As the chicken cooks the liquid in the pan thickens to give the tasty sticky coating.

Serve with boiled new potatoes and seasonal vegetables.

fish and seafood

Fish and seafood are so versatile and tasty, especially when freshly caught from the sea. You'll be amazed by the variety of low-fat, easy-to-make dishes in this chapter, from Herb-crusted Haddock with Tomato Salsa to Sole and Smoked Salmon Rolls. Eating well has never been so rewarding.

very easy

prep 10 mins

cooking 10–15 mins

herb-crusted haddock with tomato salsa

115 g/4 oz fresh white breadcrumbs

3 tbsp lemon juice

1 tbsp pesto sauce

2 tbsp chopped fresh parsley

salt and pepper

vegetable oil spray

4 haddock fillets

1 tub tomato salsa, to serve

SERVES 4

Put the breadcrumbs, 2 tablespoons of the lemon juice, the pesto sauce, parsley, salt and pepper in a bowl and mix well together.

Line a grill pan with aluminium foil and spray with vegetable oil. Place the haddock fillets on the foil and sprinkle with the remaining tablespoon of lemon juice, more salt and pepper and cook under a preheated grill for 5 minutes.

Turn the haddock fillets over and spread the herb and breadcrumb mixture over the top of each.

Cook for a further 5–10 minutes, or until the haddock is tender and the crust is golden brown.

Serve with the tomato salsa spooned over the top of each fish.

NUTRITIONAL INFORMATION	
calories	245
fat	2g
saturates	0g

seafood pizza

easy

prep 25 mins +
1 hr rising

cooking 55 mins

140 g/5 oz standard pizza
  base mix

4 tbsp chopped fresh dill or
  2 tbsp dried dill

fresh dill, to garnish

SAUCE

1 large red pepper

400 g/14 oz canned chopped
  tomatoes with onion and
  herbs

3 tbsp tomato purée

salt and pepper

TOPPING

350 g/12 oz assorted cooked
  seafood, thawed if frozen

1 tbsp capers in brine,
  drained

25 g/1 oz stoned black olives
  in brine, drained

25 g/1 oz low-fat mozzarella
  cheese, grated

1 tbsp freshly grated
  Parmesan cheese

NUTRITIONAL INFORMATION	
calories	248
fat	6g
saturates	2g

SERVES 4

Place the pizza base mix in a large bowl and stir in the dill.
Make the dough according to the packet instructions.

Press the dough into a round measuring 25 cm/10 inches
across on a baking sheet lined with baking paper. Leave to
rise for 1 hour, or until doubled in size.

Preheat the oven to 200°C/400°F/Gas Mark 6. Preheat the
grill to hot. To make the sauce, halve and deseed the pepper
and arrange on a grill rack. Cook under the preheated hot
grill for 8–10 minutes, or until the flesh is soft and the skin is
blackened and blistered. Leave to cool slightly, then peel off
the skin, chop the flesh and place in a saucepan with the
tomatoes. Bring to the boil and simmer for 10 minutes. Stir in
the tomato purée and season to taste with salt and pepper.

Spread the sauce over the pizza base and top with the
seafood. Sprinkle over the capers and olives, top with the
cheeses and bake in the preheated oven for 25–30 minutes.
Garnish with sprigs of dill and serve hot, cut into slices.

very easy

prep 5 mins

cooking 15 mins

linguine with prawns

350 g/12 oz linguine

salt and pepper

1 tbsp white wine vinegar

1 tbsp lemon juice

2 tbsp tomato purée

pinch of sugar

6 tbsp water

1 tsp chopped fresh garlic

1 tsp chopped fresh ginger

225 g/8 oz shelled cooked
    prawns

4 spring onions, sliced thinly

chopped fresh parsley,
    to garnish

SERVES 4

Cook the pasta in a large saucepan of boiling salted water for
10 minutes, or as directed on the packet, until tender.

Meanwhile, put the vinegar, lemon juice, tomato purée, sugar,
water, salt and pepper in a bowl and mix together.

Put the garlic, ginger, prawns and spring onions in a large
non-stick frying pan and heat for 1–2 minutes, stirring all the
time, until hot.

Drain the cooked pasta and add to the frying pan. Mix into the
sauce mixture and heat, stirring, until the pasta is well coated
and the sauce is heated through.

Serve garnished with chopped parsley.

NUTRITIONAL INFORMATION	
calories	359
fat	2g
saturates	0g

kedgeree

225 g/8 oz haddock fillet

225 g/8 oz smoked haddock
  fillet

1 tbsp sunflower or corn oil

1 onion, chopped

$1/2$ tsp ground turmeric

$1/2$ tsp ground cumin

$1/2$ tsp chilli powder

$1/4$ tsp ground ginger

225 g/8 oz long-grain rice

salt and pepper

1 hard-boiled egg and 2 tbsp
  chopped fresh parsley,
  to garnish

NUTRITIONAL INFORMATION	
calories	340
fat	5g
saturates	1g

SERVES 4

Place the haddock fillets in a large, heavy-based frying pan. Pour in enough water to cover and poach gently over a low heat for 10–15 minutes, or until the flesh flakes easily. Remove the fish with a fish slice and leave to cool. Sieve the cooking liquid into a measuring jug and make up to 600 ml/1 pint, if necessary.

Heat the oil in a flameproof casserole. Add the onion and cook over a low heat for 3 minutes, or until soft. Stir in the spices, then the rice, and cook, stirring, until well coated. Stir in the reserved cooking liquid. Bring to the boil, cover and cook over a low heat for 20 minutes, or until all the liquid has been absorbed and the rice is tender.

Meanwhile, skin the fish and remove any remaining bones, then flake the flesh. Fold the fish into the rice, season to taste with salt and pepper and transfer to a large, warmed serving dish. Shell the hard-boiled egg and cut into quarters, then use to garnish the kedgeree. Sprinkle with chopped fresh parsley and serve immediately.

easy

prep 30 mins

cooking 20 mins

sole and smoked salmon rolls

55 g/2 oz fresh wholemeal
   breadcrumbs

$^1/_2$ tsp grated lime rind

1 tbsp lime juice

55 g/2 oz low-fat soft cheese

salt and pepper

4 sole fillets, about 125 g/
   4$^1/_2$ oz each

55 g/2 oz smoked salmon

150 ml/5 fl oz fish stock

150 ml/5 fl oz low-fat natural
   yogurt

1 tbsp chopped fresh chervil

fresh chervil sprigs,
   to garnish

selection of freshly steamed
   vegetables and lime
   wedges, to serve

NUTRITIONAL INFORMATION	
calories	191
fat	4g
saturates	2g

SERVES 4

Preheat the oven to 190°C/375°F/Gas Mark 5. Mix the breadcrumbs, lime rind and juice, soft cheese and salt and pepper together in a bowl until a soft stuffing mixture is formed.

Skin the sole fillets by inserting a sharp knife in between the skin and flesh at the tail end. Holding the skin in your fingers and keeping it taut, strip the flesh away from the skin. Halve the sole fillets lengthways.

Place strips of smoked salmon over the skinned side of each fillet. Trim the salmon as necessary. Spoon one-eighth of the stuffing on to each fish fillet and press down along the fish with the back of a spoon. Carefully roll up from the head to the tail end. Place, seam-side down, in a large ovenproof dish and pour in the fish stock.

Bake in the preheated oven for 15 minutes. Using a fish slice, transfer the fish to a warmed serving plate, cover and keep warm. Pour the cooking juices into a saucepan and add the yogurt and chopped fresh chervil. Season to taste with salt and pepper and heat gently without boiling. Garnish the fish rolls with chervil sprigs and serve with the yogurt sauce, steamed vegetables and lime wedges.

vegetarian

Vegetarian food has long been the healthy option, but not the most exciting. These dishes reveal the very best in sophisticated vegetarian cuisine, suitable for any day of the week. Penne Primavera or Chinese Vegetables with Noodles would be a hit with guests, or a treat with a good glass of wine at the end of the day.

easy

prep 25 mins + 15 mins to cool

cooking 1 hr 25 mins

roasted vegetables with hot chilli pepper dip

4 tbsp olive oil

2 potatoes, about 175 g/6 oz each

2 red-fleshed sweet potatoes, about 175 g/6 oz each

1 large parsnip

6 turnips, about 85 g/3 oz each

few sprigs of fresh rosemary

2 garlic cloves, crushed

2 courgettes

1 aubergine

FOR THE DIP

3 fresh red chillies, sliced

1 red pepper, deseeded and finely diced

1 onion, finely chopped

400 g/14 oz canned chopped tomatoes in tomato juice

100 ml/3^1/$_2$ fl oz vegetable stock or cold water

SERVES 4

Preheat the oven to 220°C/425°F/Gas Mark 7. Divide the oil between 2 large roasting tins and heat in the oven.

Scrub the potatoes and cut into wedges. Peel the parsnip and turnips. Cut the parsnip into strips about the same size as the potato wedges. Cut the turnips in half. Cook in a large saucepan of boiling water for 5 minutes, drain well and carefully add to the roasting tins. Using a spoon, turn and coat the vegetables with the hot oil. Divide the rosemary and garlic between the roasting tins and roast in the preheated oven for 15 minutes.

Cut the courgettes and aubergine into long chunks, just slightly larger than the potato wedges. Remove the roasting tins from the oven and divide the courgettes and aubergine between them, carefully tossing them in the hot oil. Roast for a further 45 minutes–1 hour, turning occasionally so that they roast evenly.

Meanwhile, make the dip. Reserve a few chilli slices for garnish and put the remainder into a saucepan with all the remaining dip ingredients. Bring to the boil, then reduce the heat, cover and simmer for 20 minutes until the onion is tender. Leave the dip to cool for 15 minutes, then process in a food processor or blender in small batches, until smooth. Return the dip to the saucepan and heat through thoroughly just prior to serving.

Pour the dip into 4 individual serving dishes, garnish with the reserved chilli slices. Divide the roasted vegetables between warmed serving plates. Serve immediately.

NUTRITIONAL INFORMATION	
calories	443
fat	15g
saturates	0.2g

chinese vegetables and beansprouts with noodles

1.2 litres/2 pints vegetable stock

1 garlic clove, crushed

1-cm/¹/₂-inch piece fresh root ginger, finely chopped

225 g/8 oz dried medium egg noodles

1 red pepper, deseeded and sliced

85 g/3 oz frozen peas

115 g/4 oz broccoli florets

85 g/3 oz shiitake mushrooms, sliced

2 tbsp sesame seeds

225 g/8 oz canned water chestnuts, drained and halved

225 g/8 oz canned bamboo shoots, drained

280 g/10 oz Chinese leaves, sliced

140 g/5 oz beansprouts

3 spring onions, sliced

1 tbsp dark soy sauce

freshly ground black pepper

NUTRITIONAL INFORMATION	
calories	336
fat	5.8g
saturates	1g

SERVES 4

Bring the stock, garlic and ginger to the boil in a large saucepan. Stir in the noodles, red pepper, peas, broccoli and mushrooms and return to the boil. Reduce the heat, cover and simmer for 5–6 minutes, or until the noodles are tender.

Meanwhile, preheat the grill to medium. Spread the sesame seeds out in a single layer on a baking sheet and toast under the preheated grill, turning to brown evenly – watch constantly as they brown very quickly. Tip the sesame seeds into a small dish and set aside.

Once the noodles are tender, add the water chestnuts, bamboo shoots, Chinese leaves, beansprouts and spring onions to the saucepan. Return the stock to the boil, stir to mix the ingredients and simmer for a further 2–3 minutes to heat through thoroughly.

Carefully drain off 300 ml/10 fl oz of the stock into a small heatproof jug and reserve. Drain and discard any remaining stock and turn the noodles and vegetables into a warmed serving dish. Quickly mix the soy sauce with the reserved stock and pour over the noodles and vegetables. Season to taste with pepper and serve immediately.

very easy

prep 10 mins

cooking 20 mins

penne primavera

115 g/4 oz baby sweetcorn

115 g/4 oz whole baby
  carrots

salt and pepper

175 g/6 oz shelled broad
  beans

175 g/6 oz whole green
  beans, cut into 2.5 cm/
  1 inch pieces

350 g/12 oz penne

300 ml/10 fl oz low-fat
  natural yogurt

1 tbsp chopped fresh parsley

1 tbsp snipped fresh chives

a few chives, to garnish

SERVES 4

Cook the sweetcorn and carrots in boiling salted water for
5 minutes, or until tender, then drain and rinse under cold
running water. Cook the broad beans and green beans in
boiling salted water for 3–4 minutes, or until tender, then
drain and rinse under cold running water. If preferred, slip the
skins off the broad beans.

Cook the pasta in a large saucepan of boiling salted water for
10 minutes or as directed on the packet, until tender.

Meanwhile, put the yogurt, parsley, snipped chives, salt and
pepper in a bowl and mix together.

Drain the cooked pasta and return to the pan. Add the
vegetables and yogurt sauce, heat gently and toss together,
until hot.

Serve garnished with a few lengths of chives.

NUTRITIONAL INFORMATION	
calories	398
fat	3g
saturates	1g

vegetable biryani

very easy

prep 10 mins

cooking 30 mins

1 onion, quartered

2 garlic cloves

1 tsp chopped ginger

1 tsp ground coriander

1 tsp ground cumin

1 tsp ground turmeric

$^1/_2$ tsp chilli powder

salt and pepper

1.4 litres/$2^1/_2$ pints water

2 carrots, sliced thickly

225 g/8 oz whole green
    beans, cut into 2.5 cm/
    1 inch lengths

$^1/_2$ cauliflower head, cut into
    florets

350 g/12 oz basmati rice

2 whole cloves

$^1/_4$ tsp cardamom seeds

2 tbsp lime juice

chopped fresh coriander,
    to garnish

SERVES 4

Put the onion, garlic, ginger, coriander, cumin, turmeric, chilli, salt and pepper in a food processor and blend until smooth.

Spoon the spice mixture into a large non-stick saucepan and cook, stirring, for 2 minutes. Stir in 850 ml/$1^1/_2$ pints of the water and bring to the boil. Add the carrots, beans and cauliflower and simmer for 15 minutes, or until tender.

Meanwhile, put the rice in a sieve and rinse under cold running water. Put in a saucepan with the remaining 600 ml/1 pint of water, the cloves, cardamom seeds and salt. Bring to the boil, then simmer for 10 minutes, or until just tender.

Drain the rice and stir into the vegetables with the lime juice. Simmer gently until the rice is tender and the liquid has been absorbed. Serve garnished with coriander.

very easy

prep 15 mins

cooking 10 mins

glazed vegetable kebabs

150 ml/5 fl oz low-fat
  natural yogurt

4 tbsp mango chutney

1 tsp chopped garlic

1 tbsp lemon juice

salt and pepper

8 baby onions, peeled

16 baby sweetcorn, halved

2 courgettes, cut into
  2.5 cm/1 inch pieces

16 button mushrooms

16 cherry tomatoes

salad leaves, to garnish

SERVES 4

Put the yogurt, chutney, garlic, lemon juice, salt and pepper in a bowl and stir together.

Put the onions in a saucepan of boiling water. Return to the boil, then drain well.

Thread the onions, sweetcorn, courgettes, mushrooms and tomatoes alternately on to 8 metal or bamboo skewers.

Arrange the kebabs on a grill pan and brush with the yogurt glaze. Cook under a preheated grill for 10 minutes, turning and brushing frequently, until golden and tender.

Serve with a garnish of mixed salad leaves.

NUTRITIONAL INFORMATION	
calories	144
fat	1g
saturates	0g

sweet
treats

The days of low-fat,

no-fun food are over and

this chapter welcomes

the most delectable of

treats, all with less than

6g of fat. Paradise! Try cool

Melon and Ginger Sorbet

for a chic dessert, or

Chocolate Pear Roulade

for a taste sensation.

extremely easy

prep 10 mins

cooking 0 mins

melon and ginger sorbet

1 ripe melon, peeled, deseeded and cut into chunks

juice of 2 limes

1 tbsp grated fresh root ginger

4 tbsp unrefined caster sugar

1 egg white, lightly whisked

fresh strawberries or raspberries, to serve

SERVES 4

Put the melon, lime juice and ginger into a food processor or blender and process until smooth. Pour into a measuring jug and make up to 600 ml/1 pint with cold water.

Pour into a bowl and stir in the sugar. Beat in the egg white.

Transfer to a freezerproof container and freeze for 6 hours.

Serve in scoops with strawberries or raspberries.

NUTRITIONAL INFORMATION	
calories	141
fat	0.4g
saturates	0.1g

apple strudel with warm cider sauce

easy

prep 25 mins

cooking 15–20 mins

8 crisp eating apples

1 tbsp lemon juice

85 g/3 oz sultanas

1 tsp ground cinnamon

$^1/_2$ tsp grated nutmeg

1 tbsp soft light brown sugar

6 sheets filo pastry

vegetable oil spray

SAUCE

1 tbsp cornflour

450 ml/16 fl oz cider

icing sugar, to serve

NUTRITIONAL INFORMATION	
calories	283
fat	1g
saturates	0g

SERVES 2–4

Preheat the oven to 190°C/375°F/Gas Mark 5. Line a baking sheet with non-stick liner.

Peel and core the apples and chop them into 1 cm/$^1/_2$ inch dice. Toss the pieces in a bowl, with the lemon juice, sultanas, cinnamon, nutmeg and sugar.

Lay out a sheet of filo, spray with vegetable oil and lay a second sheet on top. Repeat with a third sheet. Spread over half the apple mixture and roll up lengthways, tucking in the ends to enclose the filling. Repeat to make a second strudel. Slide on to the baking sheet, spray with oil and bake for 15–20 minutes.

Blend the cornflour in a pan with a little cider until smooth. Add the remaining cider and heat gently, stirring all the time, until the mixture boils and thickens. Serve the strudel warm or cold, dredged with icing sugar and accompanied by the cider sauce.

easy

prep 40 mins

cooking 10 mins

chocolate pear roulade

sunflower oil, for oiling

40 g/1½ oz plain flour

15 g/½ oz cocoa powder,
   plus 1 tsp for dusting

2 eggs

85 g/3 oz caster sugar

1 tbsp hot water

1 orange, halved

2 ripe pears

200 g/7 oz low-fat fromage
   frais

SERVES 4–6

Preheat the oven to 200°C/400°F/Gas Mark 6. Line a 27- x 17-cm (10¾- x 6½-inch) Swiss roll tin with greaseproof paper and oil very lightly.

Sift the flour and cocoa powder together into a mixing bowl.

Put the eggs and sugar into a warmed, heatproof glass mixing bowl and whisk until pale in colour and a trail is left when the whisk is lifted out of the mixture. This will take approximately 15 minutes if using an electric hand mixer. (If using a manual hand mixer, the mixture can be whisked over a saucepan of hot but not boiling water to help reduce the whisking time.)

Carefully fold the flour mixture into the whisked egg mixture using a metal tablespoon. Stir in the hot water. Pour the mixture into the prepared tin and gently tilt to level the mixture. Bake in the preheated oven for 8–10 minutes, or until the point of a sharp knife inserted into the centre of the sponge comes out clean.

Turn the sponge out on to a sheet of greaseproof paper placed over a clean tea towel. Carefully peel the lining paper off the sponge and trim any crisp edges with a sharp knife.

Using the greaseproof paper under the sponge, loosely roll up the sponge from the short end and leave to cool completely on a wire rack.

Meanwhile, squeeze the juice from 1 orange half into a bowl. Peel, quarter and core the pears. Thinly slice and toss in the juice to prevent discolouration. Slice the remaining orange half and reserve for decoration.

Carefully unroll the cooled sponge and spread with the fromage frais, leaving a 2.5-cm/1-inch border. Drain any excess orange juice from the pears. Reserve a few pear slices for decoration and cover the fromage frais with the remaining slices. Carefully re-roll the sponge.

Using a sharp knife, slice the roulade into portions and serve on plates decorated with the reserved pear and orange slices. Lightly sift over the cocoa powder and serve immediately. This dessert is best eaten on the day it is made – any leftover roulade should be stored in the refrigerator and consumed within 24 hours.

NUTRITIONAL INFORMATION	
calories	232
fat	5.6g
saturates	1.9g

brown sugar pavlovas

2 large egg whites

1 tsp cornflour

1 tsp raspberry vinegar

100 g/3^1/$_2$ oz light
muscovado sugar,
crushed free of lumps

2 tbsp redcurrant jelly

2 tbsp unsweetened
orange juice

150 ml/5 fl oz fat-free
natural fromage frais

175 g/6 oz raspberries,
thawed if frozen

rose-scented geranium
leaves, to decorate
(optional)

NUTRITIONAL INFORMATION	
calories	155
fat	0.4g
saturates	2g

SERVES 4

Preheat the oven to 150°C/300°F/Gas Mark 2. Line a large baking tray with baking paper. Whisk the egg whites in a spotlessly clean, greasefree bowl until very stiff and dry. Fold in the cornflour and vinegar. Gradually whisk in the sugar, a spoonful at a time, until the mixture is thick and glossy.

Divide the mixture into 4 portions and spoon on to the prepared baking sheet, spaced well apart. Smooth each portion into a round, 10 cm/4 inches across, and bake in the preheated oven for 40–45 minutes, or until lightly browned and crisp. Leave to cool on the baking tray until cold.

Place the redcurrant jelly and orange juice in a small saucepan and heat, stirring constantly, until melted. Remove the saucepan from the heat and leave to cool for 10 minutes. Using a palette knife, carefully remove each pavlova from the baking paper and transfer to a serving plate. Top with the fromage frais and the raspberries. Glaze the fruit with the redcurrant jelly and decorate with the geranium leaves, if using.

index